REVERSING DECADES OF SOCIETAL DEGRADATION IN AMERICA

"A common lament of the World War II generation is the absence today of personal responsibility" Tom Brokaw

The continued erosion of American society must be reversed or future generations will place the nation at risk with providing enough quality workers to fulfill the needs of industry and quality recruits for the All-Volunteer military. The nation needs to reverse present societal trending and reform itself toward embodying the nationalistic traits and characteristics expected by the leader and example for global democratization. America's culture is in a state of moral decline, an issue that resonates both here and abroad. Continued negative trending caused by decades of societal conditioning has eroded the preparedness of America's youth and is draining its pool of qualified applicants to dangerously low levels. This includes the erosion of the foundations of family stability, the increased amount of single parented households, the breakdown of the belief in the traditional family, greatly increased use of television and electronic media, and the amount of time children are left alone without parental supervision. Further, the globalization of America as a networked society has reduced nationalistic sentiments once greatly valued by previous generations which strove to perform as the world's example for virtuous society. These disturbing trends on obesity, other health issues, and an overall lowered intellectual prowess leads to the fact that America must enact societal reform now to ensure future generations are fully prepared to meet its internal demands while serving as the leader of the free world. It is time for the birth of a new era, one I will call the Progressive Era of Reform. I view this era as a tempered combination of the ideals for social activism, political and civil reform, and individual enlightenment that is drawn partly from the Era of Reform from the early 1800's, but primarily from the Progressive Era (minus prohibition) of the early 1900's. It is time for a return to the challenge President John F. Kennedy proposed to the nation during his inaugural address on January 20, 1961 when he called on Americans to commit to service and sacrifice as noted in the following excerpts from a speech that resonates closely with today's degraded societal virtues.

> *"We dare not forget today that we are the heirs of that first revolution. Let the word go forth from this time and place, to friend and foe alike, that the torch has been passed to a new generation of Americans - born in this century, tempered by war, disciplined by a hard and bitter peace, proud of our ancient heritage - and unwilling to witness or permit the slow undoing of those human rights to which t his Nation has always been committed, and to which we are committed today at home and around the world.*
>
> *And so, my fellow Americans: ask not what your country can do for you - ask what you can do for your country.*
>
> *My fellow citizens of the world: ask not what America will do for you, but what together we can do for the freedom of man.*
>
> *Finally, whether you are citizens of America or citizens of the world, ask of us the same high standards of strength and sacrifice which we ask of you. With a good conscience our only sure reward, with history the final judge of our deeds, let us go forth to lead the land we love, asking His blessing and His help, but knowing that here on earth God's work must truly be our own."*[1]

In 2011, Americans conducted remembrance ceremonies marking the tenth anniversary of the September 11, 2001 terrorists attacks that killed 2,977 people, destroyed the World Trade Center Towers, crashed a commercial airliner into a Pennsylvania field, and severely damaged the Pentagon while striking directly into the heart of our nation's capital. These awful attacks committed untold damage to the country's psyche while showing an unforeseen vulnerability to the world.[2] While visiting the fractured and rubbled grounds of the World Trade Center just days after the attack,

President George W. Bush exclaimed to an emotionally charged crowd of rescue workers, "I can hear you. The rest of the world hears you. And the people who knocked these buildings down will hear all of us soon."[3] President Bush subsequently ordered the U.S. Military into action in Afghanistan on October 7th, 2001 and into what has become the longest war in American history outside of the Cold War.

Following the terrorist attacks, the U.S. Military quickly mobilized and prepared to fight with the force structure and equipment it had on hand. There was no time to create the "ideal" or "perfect" Soldier, weapon, or fighting formation to counter an asymmetric and largely unseen foe that was located half-way around the world. The nation went to war fighting with a military that had been developed and trained during the mid to late 1990s and structured to fight a traditionally symmetrical threat such as another conventionally structured state-led military. This was the post-Operation Desert Storm downsized military force structure that had participated in several small scale combat, peacekeeping, and stability type operations in Somalia, Haiti, Bosnia and Kosovo.[4] As the Global War on Terror's campaign strategy shifted from offensive to counterinsurgency operations, the military clearly needed to evolve from its 1990's methodologies. In order to effect change on this massive institution, the military changed long standing bureaucratic policies that added the ability to quickly right-size, right-equip and adapt to meet the Global War on Terror's ever changing landscape of combat, counter-terrorism, and counterinsurgency operations.

The All-Volunteer Military

Of extreme importance is the quality of recruits that willingly enlist for the All-Volunteer military, including the study of what induces them to serve and the baseline attributes that they will report to basic training. These factors affect how the institution will focus its massive human resources recruiting budgets. Assessing where to find and recruit the service members of tomorrow requires the study of generational change, and as importantly, the implications on these generations caused by decades of societal conditioning and changing societal norms. America, its culture and institutions, democratization and the free market economy were at one time viewed by the oppressed citizens of the world as an inspiring motivational catalyst for change, often at personal risk. The past fifty years of American societal changes has produced a continued declining trend on the definition and expectations of core values and beliefs that embody the meaning of living an honorable life. The past several decades of societal conditioning has cheapened the values and expectations on how American citizens are expected to perform, behave, educate, and serve themselves and the nation. These are facts that must be accounted for in the recruiting process because the All-Volunteer military equally represents the population and demographics of American culture. The All-Volunteer military must decide and develop strategies to teach, train and enforce recruits to an appropriate level on a code of values and virtues that likely does not exist in their core beliefs based on societal conditioning issues. Therefore, the U.S. Military has a role in reversing negative societal trending, and is an institution that is already equipped with proven methods that embody new recruits and serving members towards living higher baseline standards of conduct. The military has oft performed in the role of a societal Petri dish for both national policies and discussions by addressing difficult issues in areas such as racism, education, diversity, gender, promotions, pay, retirement, health care standards, gays, voting, and environmental policies.

Resulting from the lengthy and sustained duration of combat operations since 2001, the U.S. Military has ushered in a new generation of American recruits who possess differing degrees of beliefs, norms and motivations than previous cohorts. Comparing Americans raised in the mid to late 20th century with those born around the millennium poses significantly different challenges. The individual upbringing, internal beliefs and characteristics of today's recruits are simply different than the ones that went to war in 2001, or even in 2006. They respond to stimulus, orders and each other in a manner that has required institutional recognition and change to the methods of teaching, coaching, training, and leading. The recruits of today are brought up in a fully networked world that is unlike anything the recruits of the 1980's and 1990's witnessed, and who were more accustomed to a life with a hierarchal structures similar to the military.

Hiring Competition between the U.S. Military and Industry

The dwindling pool of qualified workers in America places competitive pressures on the U.S. Military and industry as they both seek to fulfill their hiring needs from the same population of 18 to 24 year olds. As a professional institution, the U.S. Military faces similar hiring challenges that American industry is dealing with when figuring out the best methods to lead, train, manage and task the recruits and workforce of today. Essential to this is realizing the scale of the total hiring needs required by these entities when compared to the shrinking pool of qualified applicants. At some point in the prerequisite employment qualifications threshold, a nexus is reached in which these institutions are staring at each other's potential hiring bin thus figuring out how to entice away qualified applicants for employment opportunities and service. As the pool of qualified applicants for the workforce continues to decline there is a heightened potential for hiring fratricide between the U.S. Military and American industry.

It Takes a Few Good Men (and Women)

Every year since 1998, Gallup Poll studies have shown the American people have expressed that they have the greatest confidence in the U.S. Military as an institution when compared with fifteen other societal level organizations.[5] With this sentiment in mind, the truth is that a great majority of Americans simply elect not to serve reality shows that less than 1% of the U.S. population is in the military today.[6] The U.S. is the world leader in military expenditures, yet it ranks eighth overall in the total number of people serving in uniform (active, reserve, paramilitary). There are 23 million military veterans in America (only 7% out of a population of 313 million) with approximately 2.5 million of them having served in combat since 9/11. America has now passed the threshold of the longest war in its history and has completed over a decade of continuous and sustained deployments supporting the war. Only 1% of the population serves on active duty at any given time, and there are only 2.5 million 9/11 veterans. These facts clearly point out that a very small percentage of the American society has been challenged to carry the nation's policy for its masses. This smacks of, "We really appreciate you being over there, and we greatly support our military, but service is really not for me or my kids." The author speaks from experience having had similar conversations during social interactions across the country. They truly don't feel the effects of the war unless they personally know a service member or hear about a casualty, beyond that it is life as usual with work, bills, vacations, etc. There is little to no direct involvement by a majority of the nation's citizens through selfless service and sacrifice that will ever result in the elimination of the radical causes or people who attacked their country on 9/11.

elitism by America's elected officials as only 20% of the 535 members of Congress having ever served in the military. This is the lowest percentage since World War II, and a far cry from the 1970's when 75% of elected officials were veterans.[8] Not a surprise when you consider only 7% of the U.S. population has ever served in the military, and that only 1% of the entire American constituency serves in the military today. This is truly an American problem when considering the importance of our elected official's ability to truly comprehend and understand how policy is developed and executed, and the military is used to best support our nation's defense. This misrepresentation must be changed by seeking opportunities that afford first person experience that is resident within the entire political staffing and decision making process. This is especially crucial for the U.S. Military when considering the fact that defense spending accounts for $553 billion of America's $3.73 trillion 2012 budget.[9]

Generational Theory

From a sociological perspective, it is also necessary to bin or cohort the potential hiring pool by generation to better understand how they think and respond to the varying stimuli of life and work. Service members that fought in 2001 were likely categorized as Generation X or Generation Y and were born from the mid-1960s to the early 1980s in the decades prior to the technological revolution. These service members possessed similar culturally ingrained beliefs regarding morals, values, and intellect that is distinctly different than today's youth. Figure 2. portrays generational birth date ranges accepted by generational theorists and method to bin the work force.

Label	Mature Generation	Baby Boom Generation	Generation X	Generation Y	Generation Z
Birth Date	1925-1945	1946-1964	1965-1980	1981-2000	2001-present

Figure 2. Generational Index[10]

The military has now shifted to recruiting Generation Z, which is also known as Generation Text, or Generation Quiet due to the fact that this cohort is the first to have grown up entirely as digital natives.[11] Clearly, different leadership and organizational methodologies and structures are required to lead the service members of today than ones that served in the mid-1990s. The military must recognize the changing needs of each generation and then evolve and change itself to best capture the necessary methods required to lead and communicate with its recruits. This issue highlights the need for the U.S. Military to continually update communications pathways and leader training to ensure there is effective multi-generational connectivity and task comprehension from leaders to subordinates for setting and carrying out orders. An example of this is to gauge the amount of verbal intent lost in translation by the methods of issuing an order directed from a thirty-five year old leader from Gen X to a service member in his early twenties who is from Gen Y. An example of this issue is captured in Figure 3., and offers interesting viewpoints codified by generational theorists while comparing the autonomous cerebral reactions by the varying generations towards external stimulus and their environment.

Views Toward	Baby Boomers (Born from 1946-1964)	Gen X (Born from 1965-1980)	Gen Y (Born from 1981-2000)
1. Level of Trust	Confident of self, not authority	Low toward authority	High toward authority
2. Loyalty to institutions	Cynical	Considered naive	Committed .
3. Most admire	Taking charge	Creating enterprise	Following a hero of integrity
4. Career goals	Build a stellar career	Build a portable career	Build parallel careers
5. Rewards	Title and corner office	Freedom not to do	Meaningful work
6. Evaluation	Once a year with documentation	"Sorry, but how am I doing?"	Feedback whenever I want it
7. Education	Freedom of expression	Pragmatic	Structure of accountability

Figure 3. Generational Index[12] **Generational difference comparisons based on 7 criteria**[13]

Looking to the future, the military must begin to think through the methods and processes required to recruit, train and lead the nation's next batch of service members, also known as Generation Always On, or the Wi-Fi babies. As an aggregate pool, this youth has only known near continuous connectivity 24/7 and 365, and are routinely devoid of personal interaction for a majority of the day. This generation has further refined and adopted their near complete reliance on digital interpersonal communications into an abbreviated form of symbolism using netspeak (howz ur day), chatspeak (get the 411, 24/7), Cyber-slang (MOS = mom over shoulder), and

Emoticons 😊 to portray terse conveyances of their thoughts and emotions. Today, the

fewest key strokes wins as one digitally multi-tasks through the sheer volume of digital

correspondence that simultaneously managed today via email, Twitter, Facebook, and

smart phones.

Several myths exist regarding who serves in military. These myths and lore are

predominantly opinions that originated from the Vietnam War's conscripted military.

Americans also derive these characterizations from after widely circulated Hollywood

movies that often portray leaders as bumbling fools and their subordinates as either

wise-guys (Stripes), get-over comedians (Gomer Pyle and MASH), drug users

(Apocalypse Now), or battle hardened and burned out combat veterans (Platoon).

Other misrepresentations include the belief that the average military member is an individual of lesser aptitude with lower formalized educational testing scores, comes from a poor and underprivileged background from our nation's inner cities, and uses the military as the stop of last resorts just short of unemployment or jail.

Reality is that 96.8% of the 2010 military recruits had a high school diploma or higher degree compared with the national populace average of 83%, which were rated highly qualified for military service based on academic certificates and testing, and come from the nation's middle class suburbia and rural households. The U.S. Military greatly values the importance of education, and statistics show that those with a high school diploma have a 70% chance of completing a three year enlistment versus a 50% likelihood for non-graduates.[15]

Studies confirm that a majority of the recruits join the U.S. Military out of their strong personal beliefs in patriotism, selfless service, and the defense of freedom and service to the nation. This core belief is less often reported on and tends to get lost in messaging due to the multitude of requirements and necessity for demographic tracking and cultural statistical analysis of the military. The southern portion of the United States provides the largest amount of recruits (42%) while also having the largest population (36%) of the 18 to 24 year-old recruiting populace. The central and the western regions of the country were nearly even in representation and provided 45% of the recruits while having 47% of the 18 to 24 year-old recruiting populace. The northeast region lags behind by only providing 13% of the recruits while having 18% of the 18 to 24 year-old recruiting populace.[16] Recruiting from upper class families was demographically proportional to its small population size. In the end, analysis shows that the myth on who services in the military is unfounded and diametrically opposed to reality. In the end, the military is underrepresented and less successful in gaining a proportional amount of recruits from lower income urban society and portions of the northeastern United States.

Figure 5. Military recruit density by region[17]

Lack in Accountability is Destroying the U.S. Society

Decades of societal conditioning and the continued degradation of social norms in U.S. has resulted in significant harmful impacts on the individual preparedness and readiness of America's youth. The varying implications of societal conditioning and changes in cultural norms over just a 15 to 30 year period has reduced the 18 to 24 year old military recruit applicant pool from 30 million to approximately 7.5 million candidates in relatively short fashion. This portrays the challenges the military faces with recruiting when considering that the entire hiring demands of the nation are competing for this small wedge of qualified applicants.[18] As the nation's youth matures, the societal conditioning issue is manifesting itself into the 18 to 24 year-old military recruit population as issues with obesity, a failing health care readiness, poor performance on military entrance exams by minorities, and criminality. Further, America is aging as the Baby Boom Generation moves toward retirement. The growth of the 18 to 24 year-old military aged recruiting population is projected to remain relatively flat over the next 30 years representing only 8 to 10% of the U.S. population, or between 26 to 32 million people with total population growth from 313 to 350 million people.[19] Alarmingly, due to the negative societal conditioning trends in America, the pool of potential recruits is reduced by a staggering 75% before ever walking into a recruiting station. This is due to a varying array of disqualifiers that make them ineligible to meet military admissions standards.

30% of the ineligibles are due to a variance of health issues including asthma, eyesight and hearing issues, autism, mental health, and attention deficit disorders. Another chunk of the ineligibles is due to overweight and obesity issues. Recruits disqualified for failing the military entrance physical exam due to obesity has increased by 70% in just fifteen years. American continues to get fatter with adult obesity rates having more than doubled since 1980, and two-thirds of the nation's adults being graded as overweight or obese. The generation after next is at risk as well as nearly 30% of the adolescent teens that fit the criterion of being overweight or obese; an issue that is trending higher with time unless something is done. This is truly a societal issue as overweight and obese teens are 70% more likely to transition into becoming overweight or obese adults, which results in another cut to the potential military recruiting pool, and an increased likelihood for significant downstream costs to the government and America's health care system. The impending catch 22 to this blooming issue is that America's ten most obese states also rank in the top quartile of our highest producing military recruiting states as well. Additionally, the continued increase in the percentage of obese and overweight minorities being ineligible for military service will affect the balance of ethnicity and diversity in the military. A 2010 Robert Wood Johnson Foundation report shows that more than 30% of the African American population in 43 states and Washington D.C. is obese, and for Latinos this includes 19 states, while in comparison to only 1 state for the white adult population (West Virginia).[20]

Criminality, though not a rising trend, still eliminates 5% of the 18 to 24 year-old potential recruit population as 1 in 10 young adults has committed a serious misdemeanor or felony offense negating their suitability to serve. Regarding education preparedness, a 2010 report by the Education Trust found that 23% out of 350,000 recruit applicants failed the Armed Forces Entrance Exam between 2004 and 2009. The Black applicant failure rate was 39%, Hispanic was 29%, while white was 16%. A secondary issue that affects successfully accepted recruits with reduced intellectual **capacities is their curtailment from access to the more specialized military positions and** occupational specialties that require higher aptitude and mental processing skills.

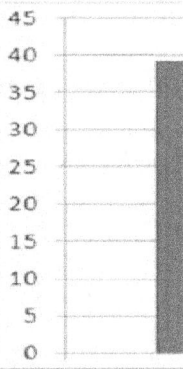

Figure 6. 2010 Armed Forces Qualification Test failure rates by race and ethnicity[21]

The minority education disqualifying issue is another implication on the potential for creating a demographic imbalance on the ethnicity and diversity in America's military, especially when coupled with the obesity and overweight disqualifying issue. If left unaddressed, both of these societal level issues pose the potential for homogenizing the military into a Caucasian formation. The obvious concern is that the future American military may not demographically look like or represent the country's population, its society, or its elected officials if these issues are left unaddressed.

Several other disturbing societal trends include the continued erosion of the "traditional" family as the number of children under the age of 18 with two parent households decreased from 69% to 66%, the number of one parent households increased from 25% to 27% (doubled since 1960), the number of unmarried couples living together rose to 7.6 million, while married couples with children decreased from 40% to 20% since 1970. This data portrays a gradually continued societal conditioning trend away from the two parent, traditionally recognized household that produced "the greatest generation."

A Society on the Matrix

Americans have also shifted from being a predominantly hierarchal society to one that is networked by nature, largely transparent, and fully connected through digital media. This includes a continued shift away from a dependence upon stationary and netwo.

Figure 7. Differences between a networked and hierarchal organization[22]

home-based electronic devices toward portable electronic gaming and music devices that provide ready and on the go access to the world wide web. Inventions that have readily curtailed the desire and need for direct interpersonal interaction have also left their mark by effectively dulling a vast societal need for non-digital social skills writ-large. The emerging generation's demand and reliance on connectivity has produced a military recruit cohort that relies on digital versus interpersonal stimulus. This is truly a generation of connectedness living continuously on the matrix that is provided by the world wide web. 91% of American's under the age of 11 are on-line, 73% of the nation's teenagers actively participate in social media, and the youth populace as a whole averages 50 hours a week on digital media devices (about half of their awake hours).

America has fully embraced and often assumed a leading role towards globalization through mass media. The implications of this include a numbing of the personal and societal beliefs and need for American nationalism. The emerging military recruit cohort lives and communicates in isolation using mass media to achieve unspoken broad communication to the masses. To better visualize the issue the author challenges the reader to attend a high school event or to ride on mass transportation and observe the nation's youth as it postures together but stares at their personal phones while texting each other for communications in close proximity versus talking to each other. 77% of American teens aged 12 to 17 have a cell phone, 75% have unlimited texting plans.[23] Teens aged 14 to 17 send on average 100 texts a day (nearly double the rate from 2008) while only 14% reported using their cell phone for a daily call to a friend.[24] This generation has completely embraced digital media to an extent that is so vastly different than how the U.S. Military has traditionally expected for its officers and non commissioned officers to lead recruits through force of personal character and personal charisma. As with any great institution, the U.S. Military will need to lead and manage change to most effectively recruit the current and emerging cohort of digitized Americans. The military will also need to assess leadership and equipping changes that must occur to best enable this generation. This will likely include the near continuous evolution in digitalization and communications medium methodologies as a potential recruiting factor to excite America's youth with access and opportunities to use cutting edge technologies.

You Can Sleep When You Die

The military should not lower or alter initial entry and recruiting standards to match the implications that the past several decades of societal conditioning has brought about as the new "norms" of American society. 9/11 served as a catalyst for mass displays of patriotism that had not been seen in America accept for brief moments that occurred at the end of Operation DESERT STORM, at the end of the Cold War, following the 1986 space shuttle disaster, and most certainly when landing a man on the moon. Unfortunately, the on-going long war has ebbed, dulled and exhausted the spirited voice of American nationalism that is so needed to wake the country from the morass of simply existing versus existing. The nation's needs a spirited voice based on virtuous challenges to spur Americans on to once again lead the world in total through example, deed, economy and military might. National leadership must seize upon this issue and inspire America to rid itself of the feeling of exhaustion. Unlike the World Wars, the nation never fully mobilized itself following the horrific unfolding of 9/11 and for the Global War on Terror. The industrial base was never placed under a national directive that dedicated its capacities toward full wartime mobilization, thus the populace was not required to ration essentials and goods and basically went on living largely in the a similar manner to the pre-9/11 days. There simply was never enough of a national demand placed upon America that warrants societal exhaustion. If any societal exhaustion exists, it is likely in America's military due to its eleven years of sustained combat operations, the myriad of endless deployments, and the internal reverberations caused to an institutional by 6,424 killed in action and another 47,545 wounded in action. The stress to force and family is a real issue and is being dealt with at the highest levels in the government and military. But, this truly only directly affects a small percentile of the total U.S. population.

General David Petraeus shared a quote that President Barack Obama made in Iraq in 2003, "He shouted to me over the noise of a helicopter before heading back to Baghdad, 'Surely, General, this is America's new greatest generation'."[26] Certainly a statement of great pride, but one that does not include the population in its entirety, as just a small percentile of America has supported the post-9/11 combat operations by either serving in the military, as contractors, in government, or for the organizations that comprise the U.S. Interagency. Also, this title is best bestowed by future historians who have gauged the achievements of this generation against the others and have based it on comparison of achievements and survivability.

Our national political process has the opportunity now to rally the nation towards the next great challenge in a similar manner that President Kennedy did in 1961. America's leadership must place a critical eye on the societal condition issues and assess where our society has evolved from, where it is today, and the trajectory it has placed itself upon supporting the nation's future endeavors. Some short term tough love from senior leadership won't win the popular vote, but it certainly could be recorded in history as the bell that tolled a sleeping giant to greatness once again, awakening a hegemony from a perceived exhaustion and spurring its population into becoming the global example of a virtuous society.

National Leadership's Role with Societal Reform

I propose that the nation's leadership identifies this national moral compass issue to America immediately, then address society in a direct manner on how it has drifted from the norms for values, conduct, accountability, and expectations of what being an American truly means. President Obama provided a point of departure with his 2010

National Security Strategy (NSS) which portrayed the United States and its people as the example and world leader for globalization and continued democratization. The NSS needs more descriptive verbiage and directness to the citizenry's individual level versus performing as an overarching societal message.[27] President Obama has provided superb guidance, but this unfortunately is at such a broad level as to be readily wished away by an individual as "someone else's issue, not mine", or never seen as a majority of the Americans will never read the NSS nor listen to messaging provided during an annual State of the Union address. According to the Nielson Ratings, only 38 million Americans watched the 2012 State of the Union address.[28] Astonishingly, nearly three times this number, or 111 million Americans watched Super Bowl XLVI just 10 days later.[29] There is something inherently wrong with society when it does not reserve the time to listen to their own President as he charts its way ahead.

National leadership must educate the nation now by resetting standards and expectations of personal conduct, accountability, values and ethos. There will be a section of the American populace that will view this as an unjustified reproach, a violation of their constitutional rights, who will both mentally and physically protest this reform. Regardless, place the requirement upon the nation and repeat it often with fact based analysis, and with time change will occur both within the individual and the society. Education, oft annunciation of, and examples by our national leadership will set the tone for expectations. Unique to the United States as a melting pot, this reform toward nationalism and a virtuous society won't fulfill itself as a repeating prophecy similar to the megalomaniacal and egocentric nationalistic evils of 20th century Germany. In other words, don't fear it, grasp upon it and live the message daily.

U.S. Military's Role with Societal Reform

The U.S. Military as a profession, possesses the authority for internal regulations and policies on policing and providing the expectations for individual conduct that exists over and above those provided by U.S. law. These regulations and policies provide a common standard for all service members regarding the expectations on values, ethos and traditions of the military as a profession. The military recruits citizens from all walks of life and coming from varying demographics, ethnicities, basis of beliefs, values, and morals. Therefore, these regulations are essential with setting the standard for ensuring all service members know what is expected of them every day both while on or off duty. Based upon their upbringings, it is fully expected that service members will need to be educated toward a common standard and expectation for personal conduct, values, and ethos. This is a learning process that continually seeks to educate a service member both personally and professionally toward embodying values that simply may not exist in the demographic of society they were raised within. The end state is for them to co-opt, live and uphold standards of conduct and values that did not previously exist in them or were not enforced as core beliefs during their youth, but are an essential embodiment of the U.S. Military profession. Service members receive recurrent training during their entire career on knowing, living and upholding the expectations of conduct, morals, values, and ethos required to be in the U.S. Military profession of arms. Certainly, this is a deep pool of talent to harness as an example, and an institution that already has an established process capable of effectively messaging, leading, and training millions of Americans in uniform who span at least two societal generations and come from all U.S. demographics. Figure 9. portrays examples of a U.S. Military institutional values and ethos code of conduct that is expected to be learned, lived and

upheld to be a successful and serving representative of the U.S. Army.

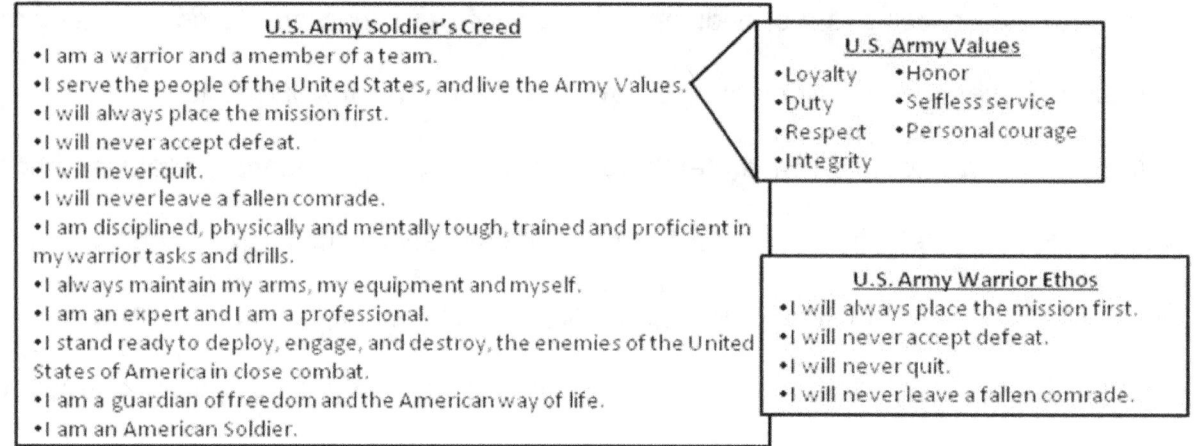

Figure 9. Examples of Institutional Values, Ethos, and Creeds (U.S. Army)[30]

The U.S. Military must have a stake in reversing the societal conditioning issue to

ensure America is prepared to provide a stable force of fully qualified recruits. The

military must continue to position itself for access into America's fully qualified work

force to hire those willing to serve based upon patriotic sentiments, a professionalized

calling, or the chance for personal economic or societal betterment.

There are several other areas the U.S. Military could partner with America's

leadership and communities while aiding with a nationally led initiative to reverse

negative societal conditioning trending including expanding the resourcing and merit of

importance of the nation's Junior Reserve Officer Training Corps (JROTC)

detachments. "Title 10 of the U.S. Code declares that 'the purpose of Junior Reserve

Officers' Training Corps is to instill in students in United States secondary educational

institutions the value of citizenship, service to the United States, personal responsibility,

and a sense of accomplishment.'" JROTC detachments are presently located in 1,645

schools and in every state and possess a cadre of 4,000 professional instructors and mentors comprised of retired military members who oversee 281,000 cadets. Additionally, the U.S. Military should seek to develop cooperative agreements for the JROTC cadre to provide values and ethics based mentorship and discussions to the high school student body.[31] This group of professionalized experts already resides in our communities, along with approximately 1.4 million National Guard and Reserve service members who could potentially aide with addressing the issue as well.

Regarding the concern surrounding an issue with civil military relations and the growing gap of America's elected officials who have not served (only 20% of the 535 members of Congress), I propose the development of an Ombudsman Program comprised of military retirees and veterans and placed under the oversight of the Secretary of Defense. It will truly perform as a return on investment for America by placing fully trained and proven stewards of ethos, values, and ethics within the national political process. This program will serve to marry up veterans of America's most favored institution, the military, with those working daily in its least favored institution, the Congress, and as rated by Gallup Polling in 2010 when Congress earned a 30 year low job approval rating of just 13%.[32] The Ombudsman Program will infuse a significant voice of military experience into the political process potentially mitigating the significant lack of military experience in America's government. This Ombudsman Program can provide a method to alleviate some of military veterans' unemployment issue which is presently at 12% and well above the national average of 8.5%.[33]

Conclusion

Reversing decades of negative societal conditioning requires purposeful and forceful leadership willing to converse on a common message that must last beyond the next bout of elections. There is personal and political party level risk in carrying such messaging, therefore this must transcend both by becoming a nationalistic objective. The key is developing a message that connects across the human, spiritual, political, and intellectual capital bases of America as being genuine, understandable, and important for both the individual and societal future of America. In the end, cultural and social renewal requires the will of the people and cannot, unlike the military, be effectively directed by a set of laws or by constitutional amendment, and would simply sit as unenforceable. To reverse course will require the nation's populace to willingly grasp the importance of the issue, agree with it, place effort and emphasis towards it. America's citizenship will also need to have a change of heart and mind while consciously and subconsciously choosing a more virtuous individual and societal pathway toward lifestyle choices and behavior. I propose that a national delegation be established and co-chaired by General (retired) David Petraeus and the former Secretary of State Condoleezza Rice to lead the development of a strategy that supports America's entry into the Progressive Era of Reform. Finally, I offer figure 10. as an example for a national code of personal and societal conduct.

American Creed of Values and Ethos

- I faithfully represent the people of the United States.
- I am a guardian of freedom and the American way of life.
- I believe in family enrichment, personal fitness, and financial responsibility.
- I believe in truthfulness, personal integrity, and respect toward others.
- I believe in continued education, diversity, and equality.
- I will live within my financial means and live responsibly for myself and others.
- I am accountable to the nation, to my neighbors and to myself for my conduct.
- I will seek the highest levels of personal conduct for myself and my family.
- I believe in service to the nation and service to others.
- I am proud to be an American and a Patriot of our nation.

Figure 10. Author's proposal of an American Creed of Values and Ethos

Endnotes

[1] The John F. Kennedy Presidential Library and Museum. Retrieved February 2, 2012 from http://www.jfklibrary.org/Asset-Viewer/Archives/JFKPOF-034-002.aspx

[2] The 9/11 Commission Report, July 22, 2004. Retrieved January 30, 2012 from http://www.9-11commission.gov/report/911Report.pdf

[3] CNN, *President Tours New York Devastation*, September 14, 2001. Retrieved on February 7, 2012 from http://articles.cnn.com/2001-09-14/us/america.under.attack_1_world-trade-center.

[4] Nina M. Serafino, *Peacekeeping and Related Stability Operations: Issues of U.S. Military Involvement, January 24, 2007.* Congressional Research Service Report for Congress. Retrieved on February 2, 2012 from http://www.fas.org/sgp/crs/natsec/RL33557.pdf.

[5] Jeffrey M. Jones, *Americans Most Confident in Military, least in Congress.* Gallup Poll Politics. Retrieved February 18, 2012 from http://www.gallup.com/poll/148163/Americans-Confident-Military-Least-Congress.aspx

[6] Sabrina Tavernise, *As Fewer Americans Serve, Growing Gap Is Found Between Civilians and Military*, November 24, 2011, The New York Times. Retrieved on January 3, 2012 from http://www.nytimes.com/2011/11/25/us/civilian-military-gap-grows-as-fewer-americans-serve.html.

[7] David Horsey, Los Angeles Times 2012. Retrieved on March 23, 2012 from www.latimes.com.

[8] Jennifer Rizzo, *Veterans in Congress at lowest level since World War II*, CNN U.S., January 21, 2011.

[9] Budget of the U.S. Government, FY 2012, Office of Management and Budget, (U.S. Government Printing Office). Retrieved on February 5, 2012 from http://www.whitehouse.gov/sites/default/files/omb/budget/fy2012/assets/budget.pdf

[10] Thomas C. Reeves and Eunjung Oh, *Generational Differences*, Handbook of Research on Educational Communications and Technology (Spector, Merrill, van Merrienboer, & Driscoll, 2007). Retrieved February 7, 2012 from http://it.coe.uga.edu/itforum/Paper104/ReevesITForumJan08.pdf

[11] Gregory P. Smith, *Here Today, Here Tomorrow*, (Chicago, Illinois: Dearborn Trade Publishing, 2001).

[12] Ibid

[13] Debard, R. D. (2004). Millennials coming to college. In R. D. Debard & M. D. Coomes (Eds.). *Serving the millennial generation: New directions for student services* (pp. 33-45). San Francisco: Jossey-Bass.

[14] Walt Handlesman, Newsday 2012. Retrieved on March 28, 2012 from www.newsday.com.

[15] Military Recruitment 2010, National Priorities Project, June 30, 2011. Retrieved on March 5, 2012 from http://nationalpriorities.org/en/analysis/2011/military-recruitment-2010/#top.

[16] Population Representation in the Military Services - Fiscal Year 2009 Report. Retrieved February 8, 2012 from http://prhome.defense.gov/MPP/ACCESSION%20POLICY/PopRep2009/contents/contents.html

[17] *Where does the military come from?*, The Electoral Map, March 17, 2009. Retrieved 15 February 2012 from http://theelectoralmap.com/2009/03/17/where-do-military-recruits-come-from/.

[18] Ibid

[19] United States Census Newsroom release November 3, 2011 retrieved on March 19, 2012 from http://www.census.gov/newsroom/releases/archives/families_households/cb11-183.html.

[20] F as in Fat: How Obesity Threatens America's Future. Robert Wood Johnson Foundation. Retrieved on February 23, 2012 from http://www.healthyamericans.org/report/88/.

[21] Army 2025 Title X Challenges Human Dimension and Operating Environment. Army Directed Studies Office Western Hemisphere Branch

[22] Ibid

[23] Amanda Lenhart, *Teens, Smartphones and Texting*, Pew Internet, May 19, 2012. Retrieved on April 2, 2012 from http://pewinternet.org/Reports/2012/Teens-and-smartphones/Cell-phone-ownership/Smartphones.aspx.

[24] Shaylin Clark, *Teen Texting Is On The Rise*, WebProNews- Business, March 19, 2012. Retrieved on April 2, 2012 from http://www.webpronews.com/teen-texting-is-on-the-rise-study-2012-03.

[25] David Horsey, Los Angeles Times 2012. Retrieved on March 27, 2012 from www.latimes.com

[26] David Rhode, Reuters, *The Great Debate, the 9/11 Generation*, September 8, 2011 retrieved on March 7, 2012 from http://blogs.reuters.com/great-debate/2011/09/08/the-911-generation/.

[27] National Security Strategy, May 2010, viewable at http://www.whitehouse.gov/sites/default/files/rss_viewer/national_security_strategy.pdf.

[28] 38 Million Watch President Obama's State of the Union Address, January 25, 2012. Retrieved on April 7, 2012 from http://blog.nielsen.com/nielsenwire/media_entertainment/38-million-watch-president-obamas-state-of-the-union-address/.

[29] David B. Wilkerson, *Super Bowl draws most viewers in TV history*, The Wall Street Journal-Marketwatch, Retrieved on April 7, 2012 from http://articles.marketwatch.com/2012-02-06/industries/31040869_1_super-bowl-xlvi-final-nielsen-ratings-highest-rating.

[30] Official Homepage of the U.S. Army, Army Mil Features, http://www.army.mil/values/.

[31] United States Army Junior ROTC. Retrieved on March 29, 2012 from https://www.usarmyjrotc.com/jrotc/dt/2_History/history.html.

[32] Jeffrey M. Jones, *Congress' Job Approval Rating Worst in Gallup History,* Gallop Poll, Gallop Politics. Retrieved on March 30, 2012 from http://www.gallup.com/poll/145238/Congress-Job-Approval-Rating-Worst-Gallup-History.aspx.

[33] Bernard Shushman, *Unemployment high for young US Military Veterans*, Voice of America, January 20, 2012. Retrieved on March 22, 2012 from http://www.voanews.com/english/news/usa/Unemployment-High-for-Young-US-Military-Veterans-137751768.html.